Time Paused Today

Also by Antony Fawcus and published by Ginninderra Press
Brindled Words
Gallimaufry
Written in Sand
The Ethiopian Afar
Midnight Echoes (Pocket Poets)
Storms (Pocket Poets)

Antony Fawcus

Time Paused Today

These poems are dedicated to my grandson, Henry.

Time Paused Today
ISBN 978 1 76109 304 3
Copyright © Antony Fawcus 2022

First published 2022 by
GINNINDERRA PRESS
PO Box 3461 Port Adelaide 5015
www.ginninderrapress.com.au

Contents

The Blue-ringed Octopus	9
Passion	10
The Lantern	11
The Five Stages of Man	12
The Power of D	13
The Manticore	14
Her Dear Hand	19
Love's Labour Lost	20
The Roots of Language	21
Splash!	22
The Dark Rose	23
A Thousand Paces	24
Ophelia	25
The Backsliders	26
The Poppy Bleeds	27
Escaping the Straitjacket	28
Hidden Treasure	29
Haunted by Humans	30
A Shocking Tale	31
Hope	32
The Gates of Dawn	33
Winds of Change	34
A Hopeless Case	35
Frigate Birds	36
Time Paused Today	37
My Small Boat	38
Kneel Gently	39
Static	40
Rapunzel	41
When Eagles Soar	42

The Thief of Dreams	43
Woebegone	44
Pierrot	45
Tobogganing	46
The Young Medlar	47
The Ape Considers Man	48
Out of My Depth	49
Regret	50
I See Their Eyes	51
Wonder Lust	52
In Fading Notes	53
The Passing of the Fly	54
The Graveyard	55
Out of Kilter	56
The Sea Casts Up Its Dead	57
Imagination	58
Heroism	59
An Awful Ordeal	60
The Gecko and the Dingo	61
Desire	63
Mamaragan	64
Larkin' About	65
The Road	66
Finnish	67
The Kiss	68
Deep in the Buried Heart	69
On Cherubs' Wings	70
The Waning of the Days	71
Cut Flowers	72
Heart Attack	73
The Snake	75
A Double Rainbow in New York	82

The Bee	83
Dawn at Guichen Bay	84
Sulphur-crested Cockatoos	85
The Weavers	86
The Secret of the Rose	87
The Seven-tined Stag	88
Consider the Oyster	89
Tilting at Windmills	90
When Inspiration Strikes	91
The Harp	92
Amongst the Stars	94
The Pool	95
Ruminations	96
Annealed by Fire	97
The Bells	98
The Sleeping Music	99
Night Ode	100
Beyond the Wit of Daylight Hours	101
Going Home	102
In His Own Image	103
Through Gritted Teeth	104
Sirocco	105
The Old Violin	106
When Leaves are Fish	107
Our Late Milkman	108
Those Who Watch and Wait	109
The Superb Fairy Wren	110
Brave Robert	112
The Eagle	113
Self-sufficiency	114
A Winter Gale	116
The Mermaid	117

Rainbow Lorikeets	118
Teenage Angst	119
Gungalo	120
The Duet	121
Family	122
The Blue Period	123
Paper Tigers	124
The Old Quarry	125

The Blue-ringed Octopus

Between the wild of sea and wild of land,
two boys explore the intertidal zone,
a no-man's-land of shells and bladderwrack
and thwack of languid tides on basalt rock;

a fiendish place of shifting sand and suck,
whose pools contain the glint of pretty things,
anemones and golden, five-point stars
to prod with sticks and poke with joyful glee,

sadistically, like little gods at play.
They're yet to see the smallest jewel of all,
quiescent, shy, and pressed against the shale,
its camouflage defence against the world.

Yet, under threat, its pulsing rings of blue
become intense, a glow it's well to heed.
Forget the Kraken myth, this octopus,
despite its size, dispenses certain death.

So, will they pay? Or will the seaweed swirl
perform a sleight of hand, a flim-flam trick,
to save the day and cover its retreat
into a den beneath the overhang?

Passion

I speak of one who lit my flame, desire,
a lucifer whose phosphorescent spark
ignited me. How brief was passion's fire
before I saw the blaggard's blackened heart.

His foetid stench is burning in my head,
a pain so great I cannot help but cry.
My waxen tears upwell, in runnels shed,
their flow in gargoyle shapes solidify,

and in the soot, my wickedness awakes.
The night-time wind grotesquely twists my blaze.
The flicker of my tongue is like a snake's,
from side to side with misandry it sways

to mesmerise each wayward passing moth,
consuming them in frenzied fires of wrath.

The Lantern

Reflections in the flame, I saw

a daub of life
with resonance of love,

rhythms of eternity
cavorting in the mind,

a seed dropped thoughtlessly
by a bird in flight of song

an expression of the stillness
at the heart of things,

reaching
beyond all bounds of reason:

the voice of poetry.

The Five Stages of Man

Poppin' out
Popinjay
Poppin' corks
Poppin' pills
Poppin' off

The Power of D

At times, the mind's eye gleams
with ten to the power of d,
where d is the power of dreams
too large or small to see.

They live at the edge of reason
where certainty's aslant,
and spring's an eternal season,
and the seed becomes the plant.

When dreamers turn to action,
the quantum of potential
is given greater traction,
and the results are exponential

or ten to the power of d
(expressed mathematically).

The Manticore

'Is this the land,' I asked, 'where legends roam
in gothic script with gilded curlicues,
the land where eremites eke out their tales
on vellum sheets, well stitched and leather-bound,
where monks illuminate their words with quills
plucked from the wings of ancient hippogriffs,
the mythic steeds of mage and paladin
that haunt the pages of their manuscripts?'

'It is, my lord, and I shall be your guide,
but, if you're wise, stay several steps behind.
A path of truth and righteousness exists,
but it is overgrown and hard to see,
for these are lawless lands where ignorance
and lies abound, and cruel men hold sway.'

He cast his hollow eye on my physique.
He scanned not just my body but my strength
of will and probed my inner core of faith.
I felt my heart grow cold, as though a wind
from Arctic wastes had caught me unawares.
Who is this man who strips my being bare,
with one swift glance, to penetrate my truth?

He wrapped his cloak to cover half his face
and beckoned me to follow in his steps.
At first, the path was straight, the weather fine,
and lavender perfumed the sultry air,
infusing distant hills with purple light.
We travelled miles, traversing rough terrain.
In time, those hills became a mountain range
and, after weeks of toil, we reached a gorge
whose sides were gouged from rock that glinted blue.

This spot defined the parting of our ways.
'The quest you chose starts here; it's yours alone.
I shall not cast my shadow on these lands…'
His next words fell upon the star-strewn night,
'…unless, in time of need, you summon Death.'

His image faded as he spoke those words,
and I was quite alone in days to come,
a small and puny man whose task it was
to face the manticore, a fabled beast
who dines on human flesh torn with his teeth.
and is, by all accounts, invincible.

Soon, daylight came and etched the rock with flame.
I edged along, becoming like a wraith
that slipped between the rocks with feline stealth.
I paused at times with eyes and ears alert.
Ere long, I heard a whip and sharp, pained cry
that split the air, and to the left, I spied
a gang of chain-bound men who toiled away,
extracting much-prized lazurite with picks
and heaping it in mounds before their guards.

These guards wore leather jerkins edged with gold,
that bore the crest, in blue, of Manticore.
They rode on fiery steeds that pawed the earth
with nostrils flared and well-groomed flanks aglow,
their pent-up energy like springs coiled tight.

I drew a hollow pipe out from my robe
and sent a feathered dart unerringly
into the haunch of one, a gadfly sting
that made him turn and bolt in wide-eyed fear.
The second horseman reared, his rein held short.
My next dart pierced his throat, unseating him.
Catlike, I sprang and pinned him to the ground
and flung his belt of keys towards the gang.

The mob, unleashed, advanced with ill intent.
My palm upraised, I held all back but one
who helped me strip the clothes from off his back
then bind his sunburnt limbs with whiplash cord
drawn tight to cut the flesh if he should stir.

I soon slipped on his garb and, in disguise,
Sprang to the stirrup of his stallion.
I paused to quench my fear before I spurred
to meet my doom upon the mountaintop
on which is perched the fortress all men dread.

On seeing me return with foam-flecked steed,
the sentinel on guard above the gate
gave tongue to the alarm, a tolling bell
that echoed to awake the garrison.
I called aloft and bade him let me in.
'No time to lose,' I cried. 'Make haste! Make haste!
A mighty army presses on my heel.
It's their intent to storm the citadel,
and I must warn our lord of their design.'

My nemesis was in the eastern tower,
one eye against the loophole in the wall.
He twitched his poisoned tail when I crept in
and shook his tawny mane as he turned round
exposing rows of teeth that dripped with blood.

I faced down Death and said, 'I did not call,
and you averred you would not touch this land
until I did.'

        Then Death inclined his head.
'A time will come when you will beg for me.'

Meanwhile, the manticore had use for one
who had the ear of Death and could confer
the two-edged gift of immortality,
and, in exchange, I tamed his wild ways
to make the mountains safe for men once more.

Her Dear Hand

He kissed her dear hand and stroked her dear face,
but the distance between them had now become vast.
She twisted her fingers and stared into space.

He remembered the days when they used to embrace;
his heart nearly broke when he dwelt on the past.
He kissed her dear hand and stroked her dear face,

but, try as he might, he could not efface
her lack of response, her demeanour downcast.
She twisted her fingers and stared into space.

Oh, where were the years he yearned to re-trace?
'Why is life such a bitch?' he constantly asked,
as he kissed her dear hand and stroked her dear face.

But in matters of love, we cut to the chase.
He banished self-pity and bravely held fast.
She twisted her fingers and stared into space.

Nights taunted with dreams but could not displace
his resolve to hold tight, right up to the last.
He kissed her dear hand and stroked her dear face.
She twisted her fingers and stared into space.

Love's Labour Lost

His supple arms embraced the moon,
an act that flushed her pink.
Indeed, it almost made her swoon
and brought her to the brink.

But, as he stroked her with each leaf,
she rose into the sky,
an act he found beyond belief.
'Why?' he cried. 'Oh, why?'

He could not understand the cause,
but here's the tragic crunch.
As sometimes is the case, it was
the wrong time of the month.

Two rabbits crouched beneath the scene.
The doe, who loved her buck,
was roused by bunny thoughts obscene.
He had much better luck.

The Roots of Language

How deep the roots of language grow
in this, our land;
a fibrous mesh that binds
us to the place where we were born,
a resonance that echoes through the heart
and never goes.

Rocks and sand exude
a liquid squeeze of words
as spittle moistens tongues
to lick round vowels
and form the sounds of home
that spill into the languid streams
of culture and belonging.

At length, these join to form a waterfall,
whose sparkle-shards bombard
the silent pool
with froth and splash, disturbing
turbid depths of ancient lore
with yet another layer.

Splash!

She's not quite five but what panache!
She bends her knees and crouches down,
sails through the air and makes a splash.
Dear God! I hope she doesn't drown.

She climbs up trees and has no fear.
She's not quite five but what panache!
She thinks she'll reach the stratosphere.
Dear God! I hope she doesn't crash.

She pulls her grandpa's white moustache.
The little devil! She's an imp.
She's not quite five but what panache!
(Watch yourself, you little shrimp!)

I think she's here, but then she ain't.
She's on her bike and, in a flash,
has disappeared. It makes me faint.
She's not quite five but what panache!

The Dark Rose

Today I read the words of one who loved
and lost that love to war. Her feelings tugged
my anchor with her yearning and despair,
and her dark rose brought on a silent tear.

Her love was like a brilliant gem that sparked
a flame to fill the caverns of my heart
but, when I raked the embers of the fire,
I only saw the ash of her desire.

A Thousand Paces

I wander down the years to reminisce
on milestones hid in grass and wayside weed,
the crossroads where my judgement was amiss,
when paths I took were falsely based on greed.

I planned each inch of life; the choices made
are measured now in feet that soldier on.
The milestone triumphs scored, how soon they fade,
when set against the joys that were foregone.

Now, as I march towards my thousandth month,
my shoulders bend with millstone might-have-beens,
I leave it to my children to confront
this world of dotty comms and backlit screens

whilst I devise mendacious lines of verse
behind a mask – lest I go viral first.

Ophelia

A small wind blows, and ripples spread
across the stream concealing weeds she wore,
bending blighted sedges on the shore:
grave are the sins she answered for.
These undulations splinter life. A head
with pallid, moonlit visage stares,
unseeing through the clinging, flaxen hairs
that swirl unhurriedly, like the ebb and flow of prayers.

Is this the weeping willow tree?
Was drowning her escape from destiny?

Manipulated by constraints of courtly life,
divided from herself by circumstance,
constricted by a cruel and morbid prince,
she was driven to this tragic end at last.

A small wind blows, and ripples spread.
This tragic death asserted women's rights,
foreshadowed future struggles, future plights
of troth, with women no longer bonded to obey.
Love and honour, yes – providing it's two-way.
Together take the ups and downs of fate but, without equality,
these undulations splinter life ahead.

The Backsliders

Cathedral columns soar, austere, and sombre grey.
Beyond them sings the choir, their *miserere mei*
a mournful sigh
that scarce disturbs the filtered shafts of hallowed air;
a sallow light, absorbing fervent prayer
to One on high.

The congregated souls, arrayed in Sunday best,
with rectitude stand tall, expecting to be blessed
and soon absolved.
Then, midweek sins confessed, devout in their amen,
they pledge to make amends, and leave again,
on good resolved.

Away from upright pews, they soon forget their vows.
Their consciences asleep, with Mammon some carouse,
committing sins.
These few, I fear, forget the edifice divine,
preferring bacchanal and vintage *wine*.
The Devil grins.

The Poppy Bleeds

The poppy bleeds forgetfulness. I lie
inhaling flimsy wisps of former days.
As through a veil, the fleeting shadows sigh;
their joyless whispers add to my malaise.

I wear my tasselled cap and velvet gown,
one languid hand is raised to cool my brow.
the hubble-bubble soothes. I slowly drown
in lethargy and leave the here-and-now.

Yet echoes still persist that keep in mind
your siren songs, their silken swish and sway,
most elegant and artfully designed
to lull my sense and steal my heart away.

I'm shipwrecked, on the rocks, washed up by guile,
but you could save my life with just one smile.

Escaping the Straitjacket

Regarding the sonnet, what do I find?
I am in a bind, constrained by kind.
Elizabethan roughs made Shakespeare sing
in the vernacular. Now rap's the thing

for teens, the blast – at last – go figure.
I'm bitten by its rhythm – de rigeur.
The rhyme is frosted on by cold convention –
couplets in this case – did I mention

innovation? New generations think
in terabytes of wordfill, not of ink,
camerae obscurae, pin-brain inversions,
but I'm an old hack – forgive my aspersions.

Don't ape others, monkey around instead;
innovate on old themes, then you'll be read.

Hidden Treasure

Spring's in the air but not his gait,
a pace that age has slowed of late.
The grasses here are shoulder high;
the old man baulks and gives a sigh,
yet presses on,

his goal the termite-ridden bridge
whose rotten planks along one edge
suggest a mocking, gap-toothed leer,
enough to prompt a hidden fear:
he's all alone.

He halts at this forsaken place,
his heartbeat falters for a space,
as in this wilderness there grows
a long-forgotten wayside rose,
replete with thorns.

Its buds are pink like pouting kisses
remembered as he reminisces:
love once was wild and unconstrained.
Who plants such thoughts, with what in mind?
He moves along.

Haunted by Humans

I am haunted by humans
and the strangeness of their ways;
in part bemused, yet silently amused
that Christian poets claim
a Graeco-Roman muse
inspires their verse –
clearly an oversight of Olympian proportions.
I claim the kudos
or magical glory
of my better verses
and have no hesitation in turfing out
Euterpe.

And then there is a horde,
a veritable pandemic,
of people who profess atheism
yet exclaim with ubiquitous monotony,
'Oh, my God!'
and cheerfully say Goodbye.
Bloody strange, I call it.
Yea, by Our Lady, strange.

God be with ye all.

A Shocking Tale

To get a laugh this Halloween,
I bought a hologram machine.
I thought it'd be a darn good scam
to create a scary hologram –

bats and spiders hung in space
and a dame in diaphanous lace.
The final touch, a candelabrum,
cast an eerie light across the room.

No sooner had I set the scene
and flicked the switch on my machine,
than who came in but Auntie Lynn,
glass in hand and soused in gin.

'Good God, Mabel, you don't look well,'
was what she uttered as she fell
over the holographic cable…
a shocking end to this fable.

Hope

I see behind the mask a twinkling eye,
a pinhole shining through the shroud of night,
a speck of ancient light, a mystery,
the one bright spark in all my universe,
enticing me beyond my earthbound clay,
into a land of dreams.
I call it hope.

The Gates of Dawn

Slow sings the sky its lullaby,
a star-born sigh.
It holds me in its hallowed palm.
The air is calm,
a sanctuary from day's alarm
imbued with charm.

Through mists a mystic presence flows;
my heartbeat slows.
Inhabiting eternity,
I am set free
to pass between the gates of dawn
as if reborn.

Winds of Change

I hear the wind, its cleansing breath.
'Away with death,'
it seems to say
as brown leaves sway.

It gives a tug and sets them free
of winter's tree,
transformed, at last;
tomorrow's past.

Persephone will bring fresh birth
and springtime mirth;
a warmer breeze
that also frees.

A Hopeless Case

He lies in fields of asphodel
imbued with essences sublime,
aspiring Heaven, caught in Hell,
disrobed by darkness, out of time,

embodied in alternate space,
his mind no longer cognisant,
he's unaware of his disgrace,
befuddled by intoxicant.

Circumlocutious balderdash
slips with the slobber from his lips;
his words come tumbling – some are rash,
and on his twisted tongue he trips.

What would you say, Professor Strunk?
Inebriated – or just plain drunk?

Frigate Birds

I watch the frigates wheel and gyre,
aloft upon a broad-winged bow;
they sideslip on the doldrum air

while plankton swirls a mile below.
When predators give chase and streak
beneath the phosphorescent glow,

these well-fletched arrows, black and sleek,
begin their meteoric dive
with sanguine throat and billhook beak.

The flying fish that tuna drive
break through a surface laced with pearl,
like silver bullets as they strive,

in vain, to beat the savage swirl
of vicious beaks when wings unfurl.

Time Paused Today

Time paused today while I inhaled the spring
and captured in my eye the bloom of youth,
but, as my memory of you took wing,
a bird flew by

and, with a sigh, I watched it disappear
beneath our roof. This small domestic truth
eclipsed the sun. That bird was you, last year.
I turned away.

Time paused today, a bird flew by,
and, with a sigh, I turned away.

My Small Boat

Tonight, I journey to the stars
in my small boat that has no oars,
rudderless and out of mind;
a journey of a different kind.

I set my sails, there is no wind,
yet they are full and billowing,
by darkness driven, nothingness,
an utter calm, a silk caress

that draws me on beyond life's care,
to fractal space, a crystal shower,
and, from the void, there comes a voice
most musical; a small, sweet noise.

It echoes, wordless, through the spheres;
diminishing, it disappears,
and all reverberation's still;
a glimpse of heaven – or of hell?

Kneel Gently

Kneel gently on his bones tonight,
for pity's sake.
>The worms need time.

His mortal soul has taken flight
for men could not forgive his crime.

For pity's sake! The worms need time
to suck his bones, bereft of air
for men could not forgive his crime.

I cannot fathom how they dare
to suck his bones. Bereft of air,
Floyd pled and pled…again he pled.

I cannot fathom how they dare!

We'll wreak revenge by wielding dread
(Floyd pled, and pled…again he pled).

His mortal soul has taken flight…
>We'll wreak revenge by wielding dread.

Kneel gently on his bones tonight.

Static

The crackle of static, a snaking blue flame
that leaps from the doorknob, a brief spark of pain
alive in the dryness that's taut as a wire,
a snapping synaptic, nerve endings on fire.

I've fled from the city's great seats of power
the frenzy besetting us every fourth year;
the hustings are busting, all froth and bubble
with soapbox hopefuls predicting more trouble,

political half-speak, political spin
obscuring with half-truth – election to win –
with animate spitting and pinpricks of fear,
ecstatic electrics intended to scare.

Electors are static, refusing to move,
ingrained in their prejudice, stuck in a groove;
the gramophone's going around and around
with a grating, frustrating sameness of sound,

so I've made an escape to my hidden lair
perched high in the mountain whose dry, static air
resounds with the shock of coyote's shrill barks
to vie with the thrill of these arcing blue sparks.

Rapunzel

My pen,
my princess,
my poem…
her poem.

I inked in the details,
saving her from herself,
from the mistakes I'd made
and the terrible consequences
of living.

Oh, my princess,
my princess,
where and why did you fly?

When Eagles Soar

Shadows loom when eagles soar
with pinions poised and spread for flight.
Such slow-winged power! I'm left in awe.
Shadows loom when eagles soar.
As this rapacious carnivore
seeks for prey, I cower in fright.
Shadows loom when eagles soar
with pinions poised and spread for flight.

The Thief of Dreams

Each day that dawns is but the thief of dreams,
the tattered veils of thought that drift through night.
They make good sense in sleep, though now the seams
are split, unable to withstand the light.

The weaving comes adrift like swirls of mist
that dissipate in rays of morning sun;
the mantle disappears, though strands persist
with which to build the domes of Kubla Khan.

For poets can, at times, rework remains
with careful, stitched-up words to form a quilt,
a patchwork made of fragments from their brains –
a Xanadu of pleasures that's rebuilt.

Though daylight looms, a poet still may weave
a weft of dreams from silk the moths reprieve.

Woebegone

Though idle basking may be wrong,
I long to; it's my lust.
If I were just a wobbegong,
I'd bask and not be fussed.
I'd lie upon the ocean floor
in camouflage,
a brown mirage,
(though rather large)
and just letharge,
discharge a yawn, then bask some more.

Pierrot

What are these rags of time we wear
for Carnevale's dance;
a syncopation worn threadbare
by bitter life's mischance?

Pierrot sadly pirouettes,
his steps dragged out by deep regrets,
his feelings ghostly silhouettes
of love now gone he can't forget.

A nimble, chequered knave steps in.
He steals a kiss! Oh, Harlequin!
He gorges on the fruits of sin,
departing, guiltless, with a grin.

'Farewell, sweet meat,' with joy he cries
and joins the cheerful dance,
while, with a tear, Pierrot sighs,
for he has missed his chance.

Tobogganing

The Cotswold Hills, this cameo,
the Beacon over Ivinghoe,
the Vale of Aylesbury spread below,
a treasured past, now long ago,

when in winter's swathe of snow
with our trusty steeds in tow,
wrapped in scarves, each nose aglow,
decked in gloves from Auntie Flo.

We'd race as fast as bobsleighs go,
my face as white as pastry dough,
but butterflies I dared not show,
though molehills tossed me to and fro.

No brakes, and just the dragging toe
to change my course, preventing woe.
I was the human dynamo,
full of braggadocio.

Much later, in the afterglow,
with bated breath, I kissed my beau,
underneath the mistletoe,
and that's the truth, Pinocchio!

The Young Medlar

Our medlar is a graceful tree;
she's young and lithely limbed.
The breezes tug enticingly;
she curtsies to the wind.

In spring she sports her crinkled blooms,
a feathered flounce of crepe
set dancing like the sea-tossed spume
that billows round the cape,

and with a shy, coquettish glance
she lures all passers-by.
A honeybee soon joins her dance,
alighting with a sigh.

He offers her his abdomen
and hand in marriage, too.
He lisps, as on his knee he bends,
'Give me your anther, do.'

She sprinkles him with golden dust
and presents her pistil,
His little heart, consumed in lust,
soon becomes asystole.

He lurches breathlessly away,
weighed down by bags of pollen,
a fickle man, to her dismay;
such stigma, now she's swollen.

The Ape Considers Man

When I consider man, his frontal lobe,
his mental reasoning, I stroke my chin.
What strange emotions he has wrapped in words
to please the ear and make his women blush;
what syntax woven into symmetry
and sprinkled with his quintessential dust;
what desiccated dreams, dried up and lost;
what wisdom petrified and penned in books.

Then there's the horseshoe charm; how fortunate
it lay beneath his tongue, so he could preach,
and what a case he made with verbal mist.
The palate he was born with now lies cleft
because, preferring words, he did not act,
so evolution seeks a change – of course.

Out of My Depth

There is a shore of certainty that lies
beneath my feet, the solid rocks I know
that time will grind to glinting grains of sand
sucked by the greedy waves that rise and fall

relentlessly, and in that shifting swirl,
I dip a toe while gazing out to see
what mist conceives; the fabled land beyond
each ginger step departing from the sure.

Yet, seeking that which lies beyond my ken,
I'm tempted by a soft, beguiling air
that leads me on until I'm in too deep,
and still the siren sings seduction's song.

The sea swells up in sharps and sinks in flats;
I flounder in her music as I swim.

Regret

The knowledge of death is upon me,
it's a lonely vigil I keep.
I yearn for the strength to speak strongly
before I succumb to that sleep.

The words held secret within me
are like wraiths that escape on my breath.
They speak of the love that I bear thee
as I lie in the shadow of death;

withheld when I should have spoken,
I would like to set the score straight,
though I fear that now I am broken,
my confession is come far too late.

How my days were wasted in darkness
when the chance was there to shine bright.
I now face the truth in its starkness
as the sun drains into the night.

I See Their Eyes

I see their eyes, I see their fear
and offer up a silent prayer.
Supplies of oxygen are low;
we must, we must maintain the flow.
When lips turn blue, it's hard to bear.

Each day more come. We hang in there
providing hope, though I despair
of saving them as, row by row,
                I see their eyes.

Each one alone as he lies there
and fights for breath. No one to share
those final hours before they go.
We intubate, and yet I know
their chance is slim. Life isn't fair.
                I see their eyes.

Wonder Lust

I planted on the page a ream of random words
to grow like seeds, and watered them with wonder lust –
a poet's yearning – but a pair were turned to birds
and flew away; two precious ones, released from dust.

Beyond the prison bars they flew, and I gave chase.
I heard them sing from trees, their trills a waterfall
whose splash plinked in the pool a rippled wave of lace.
A golden fish arose beneath an egret's shawl,

and her sharp beak stabbed down to pierce the pinioned thought,
whose writhing golden scales were lifted from my eye.
The cruelty reminded me that beauty's bought
at cost of life when egrets soar and fishes fly.

Yet still, my lovebirds sang to greet the coming dawn.
with stealth I crept and with a net recaptured them,
to cage them once again. No more they sing, forlorn,
for words have clipped their drooping wings. Their eyes condemn

the one who sought to scribe and pinion flight's true worth.
They scratch, uprooting all my seedlings, and I sigh.
They peck the scattered words till all that's left is earth
and my two captured birds. Then, gorged, they also die.

In Fading Notes

A ghazal

My world was held in fading notes,
all doubts dispelled in fading notes.

The joy I felt was housed in hope,
a hope that dwelled in fading notes.

I read into your words a love
unparalleled in fading notes.

Alas, the song was out of tune;
your love withheld in fading notes.

The bell was cracked and dissonant,
its discord knelled in fading notes.

The loyalty I gave was given
and not compelled in fading notes.

Diminished chords destroy Semut;
his ardour quelled in fading notes.

The Passing of the Fly

I must protest the passing of the fly.
Whereas a failing button's not too bad,
a broken zipper leaves me high and dry,

my easy-going nature goes awry.
A sticking zip's a thing that makes me mad.
I must protest the passing of the fly.

My zip derails, my wife lets out a sigh,
my children get embarrassed for their dad.
A broken zipper leaves me high and dry.

Can't close the gap, no matter how I try;
fair maidens see me blush and think me sad;
I must protest the passing of the fly.

Those teeth that nip the skin have made me cry,
I should have kept my old pants. Wish I had;
a broken zipper leaves me high and dry.

Four buttons out of five, and I'll get by;
it's buttons every time for me, my lad.
I must protest the passing of the fly;
a broken zipper leaves me high and dry.

The Graveyard

Go slow, dear life, go slow;
death's knell I hear.
Cold grey stones
in sombre rows,

a chiselled ancestry
of those who've lived
from year to year,
now free from charnel's grasp,
their lives engraved
in brief, in lichened words.

My years, too, are nearly told.
Go slow, dear life, for me;
I fear these monuments,
these ghosts, this final masonry.

Out of Kilter

Hurtling down the helter-skelter,
thoughts like quasars out of kilter.
Each kaleidoscopic pattern,
individual in its fashion.
Avalanche, confused, snow-blind,
wrenched from regions undefined,
snowflake fractals, shattered shards,
sun-glint shrapnel, jagged words
that the poet's neatly freighted,
blunted, buried, decimated.

The Sea Casts Up Its Dead

The sea casts up its dead upon the shore,
a ghastly ship, a gull weighed down with tar,
an empty carapace, dismembered claw
entwined in bladderwrack, a broken spar.

A ghastly ship, a gull weighed down with tar,
a nine-tailed cat, a blood-soaked string of beads
entwined in bladderwrack, a broken spar
remind us of the wreck and widows' weeds.

A nine-tailed cat, a blood-soaked string of beads,
a hollow bleach of bones and shattered shell
remind us of the wreck and widows' weeds.
Such flotsam shifts upon the tidal swell.

A hollow bleach of bones and shattered shell,
an empty carapace, dismembered claw;
such flotsam shifts upon the tidal swell.
The sea casts up its dead upon the shore.

Imagination

A ghosting of the life that we could lead;
this larval stage, when we accumulate,
oh, so mindlessly, we live to feed;
is this why we are here? The final state?

Consider lowly larvae that pupate
in solitude, preferring not to crawl.
It's good, at times, to stop and contemplate
the nursery world, as does Linnaeus' doll.

But then it's time to act! Imagine well!
Feel the growing chords that orchestrate
the symphony beyond our living shell,
then let us rise to find our true estate,

to soar on wings, as is our right by birth,
not in the afterlife, but here on Earth.

Heroism

Hew the heart of woodland oak
to craft a ship,
to carve a flute
to sing the unsung heroes in,
all trammels cast aside;

all those
who live at last, alive
to love and hope
in face of hate and greed,
despite all suffering.

I saw a pretty hat, a sun-flecked frock,
a withered face that wore a smile,
held nothing back,
unfettered, free
to spend life's coin
beyond reserve
before it sealed her tongue and lip.

I saw a man
who, losing all,
retained his dignity.

I looked inside
the casket
of myself
and there the acorn lay.

An Awful Ordeal

Oh, Pantygynt, our Celtic bard,
your awdl's hard to write.
I'd hoist you with your own petard,
but *merde!* It won't ignite!

> The rhymes are cross, and so am I;
> my efforts just produce a sigh,
> no matter with what will I try.

My fuses die – so trite!

Perhaps, with practice, I'll improve,
my muse will move me on,
but when I'm almost in the groove,
the cove insists I'm wrong.

> My mind's constricted by the form,
> the words that come will not perform,
> my poetry is quite forlorn.

The vision's gone! So long!

This awful Awdl's at an end;
it will not mend. I'm sad
to find my verse so poorly penned,
my friend – but also glad

> if what I've done has made you smile.
> A little humour will beguile
> the idle hour, and for a while,

I thought my style not bad.

The Gecko and the Dingo

My rhyme is of a gecko that harassed
a savage, yellow dingo,
with courage unsurpassed.
Among the *cognoscenti*
and, as you know, there's plenty
between here and Pinnaroo,
I hear there may be twenty,
give or take a few,
that, having heard my story,
vouch the tale is true.

The part that makes it famous
is that Gecko closed his anus
with a knotted piece of string,
'cos he didn't want to shame us
with a fearful squirt of poo,
and there he stood, unblinking,
his lidless eyes unwinking,
and Dingo stood there, too,
with saliva dripping
at the thought of gecko stew.

A gecko's tail's designed to fail.
In times of danger it will fall,
then wiggle, wiggle, like a worm.
The twenty *cognoscenti* say
that is because, this very day,
he tied the string a tad too tight;
it acted like a tourniquet.
As Dingo licked his lips, prepared to eat,
Gecko's tail fell at his feet.

'A snake! A snake!' He shook and quaked.
Our dingo had a yellow streak
and limbless reptiles made him freak.
What is more, the caudal failure
caused a fart that shook Australia,
and the mutt mistook for aggression
Gecko's explosive decompression,
a sound so loud, the poor dog fled.

Coda (or tailpiece)

In time, the gecko's tail regrew
and very soon was good as new.
His tail secure, my tale's no more
…and so, my child, it's time to snore.

Desire

He stirred the fire.
In turn, the fire stirred him.
At first, when warm, it did no harm,
but then it grew, as does desire.
Each hot flame licked what he mistook
for sighs. Those flames are lies,
which craftily transmute his chosen truth,
with lust consuming all he thought.
The fire subsides to ash and dust.

Mamaragan

The gentle swish of leaves when all is calm
susurrates like silk that sweeps the floor
as ladies coyly chat, without alarm,
in whispered tones, of those that they adore.

A stronger gust soon sets the leaves to dance.
They tug, as does the puppy on his leash
when winds hold tempting scents to make him prance.
They're like impatient children who beseech

their grandpa to relent and set them free.
Brisk weather such as this was made for kites.
The old man sighs. He's tempted to agree,
when with a fearsome crack, the lightning strikes.

The wind, with nostrils flared, kicks off its trace,
and weaker leaves are wrenched from flailing trees.
They whirl around, with flurries giving chase,
as towering clouds lift up the whitecap seas.

The god, with booming voice, has hurled his spear;
Mamaragan is mad and run amok.
The ancient trunk is split. The fates conspire
to pinch beneath its limbs, an ancient, broken back.

He strained with cracking bones, to hold his ground.
He'd fought the storm before and beat the fiend,
but – a gentle swish of leaves now marks his end.
Kites circle overhead, and soon will land.

Larkin' About

Just larkin' about, and playin' with rhyme
alone in the gloom, at the edge of the zone,
for regular rhyme can be rather tame.
Though purists despair, let's persist with this tune.

I disdain same-old-same for something sublime;
near-rhyme Nirvana's the meme I would claim.
Aha! Half a rhyme! The dog's found a bone!
Eschew it or chew it? My choice alone.

The poet's at best who departs from himself.
It gives you a fillip to know that you differ;
be blind to the bland that's often on offer;
depart from home shores, if you would find wealth.

The Road

The way is straight and narrow,
the destination near,
but I prefer a winding road,
an ancient road more dear.

For me, the road's what matters,
the road that hugs the hill.
When I am on the old road,
I have no fear of ill.

The hawthorn bends and beckons,
so, too, the Old Man's Beard.
This road is safe, I reckon,
but the destination's feared.

I must espouse the winding way
beyond the wicket gate,
where every footstep's heaven;
I care not if I'm late.

Finnish

She speaks with eyes of ice and tripping tongue,
a lilting poetry transposed to song.
Is this the Finnish dream bird that I hear,
who keeps the sleeper safe when nights are long?

Her language dances lightly over words
with trills and brittle consonants of frost.
I hear the kee-kee-kee of Arctic terns,
and music from old sagas not yet lost.

The scribe of Middle Earth wove elvish runes
from language forged like mithril, strong but light.
Its silver tones drew strength from days long gone;
steel threads from tales spun through the timeless night.

The Kiss

The muse abides where nature's held in time;
each figure poised in love's eternal clasp;
their balanced architecture's strong, sublime
as spires that soar from churches' heights, so vast

in concept that, when carillons ring clear,
they seem to shake the sky in sweet alarm,
awaking inspiration with their prayer
to bless such harmonies of human form.

A pair of lovers stop to gaze in awe;
their bodies tense and, with a loving glance,
their eyes connect as, shyly, they adore
and coyly osculate in resonance.

As art unites with life, expressing bliss,
true meaning is renewed in Rodin's *Kiss*.

Deep in the Buried Heart

Deep in the buried heart of all I hold,
the jumble of long years and memory,
are things once bought, not thinking what was sold
acquiring them, when simple things were free.

Though late, I've learnt to fossick and discard
these falsely valued baubles from life's hoard,
and, now I've started, find that it's not hard
to free myself from dross that I have stored.

Hid under lumber of the years I lost,
lie tattered vestiges of days like sighs,
when we gave all and did not count the cost;
when truths were still untarnished by small lies.

A good spring-clean is all it takes, it seems,
to rediscover long-forgotten dreams.

On Cherubs' Wings

I imagine, arms outstretched, I embrace
the very essence of the artist's oils
as paint dissolves in swirls of pulsing grace,
freed from the gilt of gesso-bordered walls.

These cherubim are poised on fragile wings
to fly towards the welcome of my arms,
and gently lift me up, a heart that sings
and soars beyond the realms of earthbound qualms.

In time I'll ask them back with me to earth,
where we will paint the city pavements gold,
and fill the hearts and souls of men with mirth,
instilling joy in all, both young and old.

The Waning of the Days

I call upon the goddess, deathly pale,
to guide me through the forests that I've dared,
and give me strength to fight against the weird
who draws me from myself, into the void.

Yet, in seeking help, I know full well,
in time her shape will change, consuming me,
and, though her gift of birch to beat the fiend
will make me clean, I too will start to fade
by autumn's equinox, when she-wolves howl
and trees withdraw their precious chlorophyll.

Though death would seem to gain ascendency,
defeating hope with slowly waning light,
the goddess quickens life in dormant seeds
implanted during spring – once more to bleed.

Cut Flowers

What murders we commit with secateurs
to captivate our objects of desire.
When blooms are cut an inner death occurs;
we stem the flow of sap, and quench the fire.

If angels' wings are clipped, they cease to fly;
our flowers, too, will wilt and colours fade,
when severed from the roots they're nourished by.
That kind of love is just a masquerade.

The blossoming of love is best enjoyed
when it's allowed to grow, from seed to seed,
for nature's precious cycle is destroyed
when youth alone is plucked, to sate our greed.

You'll find there's more to love than meets the eye;
the plant itself needs nurture, lest it die.

Heart Attack

A hooded stranger pulled the cord;
he paid the fine,
and beckoned me
to leave the train
for realms I did not know.
I did as I was bid.

It was a sunny day,
breezes swayed the aspen leaves,
and teased the golden corn,
and cooled my brow.

In time, the road became more steep;
my breath less sure.
The track pressed in
until its margins disappeared,
and I was left alone,
with just the sun, the breeze,
and a spectre
overhead.

I was transfixed, and mesmerised
by its fluttering form,
and sank into the meadow grass,

yet thought the hawk
too high and small a thing
to bother me,
until, with folded wings, it fell
unerringly,
extending claws to crush
its tiny pulsing prey.

With that,
the watching stranger smiled,
and slowly walked away.

The Snake

A Crown of Heroic Sonnets

1

This snake that came was only seeking life.
Each flicker of his tongue could smell the air;
a sense that's honed to sharpness like a knife,
to slice the still of night and lay it bare,

but stones were loose and, as he was near blind,
they caused his fall into my stagnant well,
whose seven frogs had piqued his hungry mind.
Trapped in an oubliette, a concrete cell

three metres deep, with sides that were so sheer
there was no way that he could scale the walls,
he splashed and flailed about in coils of fear,
as we are apt to do when woe befalls

and sets us panicking. Around, around
the foursquare cell he swam, to seek an out,
but there was none. With fading hope, he found
his fate was sealed; of that, he'd little doubt.

So, on this night, my metaphor was born
as I got up to greet the coming dawn.

2

As I got up to greet the coming dawn,
I cleansed my thoughts and climbed the higher path,
above the well, but found my senses drawn
towards a sudden ebony of wrath

that swirled up from the depths and made me start.
The redness of his belly was exposed
and his forked tongue held lies to tear apart
my reason, with misgivings undisclosed.

Malevolently, we met each other's gaze;
our venom sacs were filled with conjoint hate,
or was it fear – the core of my malaise?
My instinct was for death, to desecrate

this helpless snake that swirled around the pool.
My firm intent; to shoot or let him drown.
One way was swift and sure; the other, cruel.
Just then he struck, and gulped the first frog down.

I saw his native instinct to survive,
digesting what it takes to stay alive.

3

Digesting what it takes to stay alive
now made me hesitate to do him harm.
He'd food enough at hand to let him thrive
And, on a beam, a place of rest and calm

for basking in the noonday hours of heat,
as I had, too; imprisoned by my thoughts,
constrained by age – though not by walls – replete
in my small world, with freedom still – of sorts.

When my small store is gone, I will expire,
a fate I thought perhaps we two could share;
two souls with stores of poison, eyes of fire,
impotent now to make our prey beware,

except of course the frogs (reduced to four).
I should forgive him that, his native bent,
for I, like him, am often carnivore
and when there's meat nearby, I am content.

We share some common features, I'll allow,
so I play god and let him live – for now.

4

So I play god and let him live for now.
(Forgive the repetition. I am old!)
Where was I in this tale of woe, and how
will these events that I relate unfold?

Ah yes – the sticking point is one of age.
This snake is in his prime, a metre long,
and yearns to roam the world beyond his cage.
He feels vibrations in a heart that's strong,

but soon his frogs will end. So, will he starve?
Unless I intervene, this snake is dead.
My hesitation, based on fear, might halve
his span of years. Yet I am filled with dread.

If I should lift him in a landing net
and scoop him up, at arm's length, on a pole,
I'd be a fool. His freedom I'd regret,
if he should strike my body from my soul.

With one false move, I'm in a six-foot plot.
On second thoughts, I think I'd rather not.

5

On second thoughts, I think I'd rather not
take such a chance. False reasons now dictate
I'll leave him there and let the devil rot
within my mind, his chosen pit; my fate.

But when a source of evil enters thought,
and settles there to fester and pollute,
our inner peace remains disturbed, and fraught
with guilt that, over time, becomes acute.

Our prejudice is apt to lead astray;
and what we think is evil may be good,
submerged in fear. There is a better way
for those who play at god. A good god would

extend a helping hand and rescue him.
I therefore call a service that saves snakes.
The price that's quoted puts me in a spin;
I baulk at saving souls for such high stakes.

The catcher has a heart to set him free;
she settles, bless her, for a lesser fee.

6

She settles, bless her, for a lesser fee;
within the hour she brings a hempen pouch,
and not much else, except the guarantee
of youth and confidence. For those, I'll vouch.

The ladder I provide is soon unfurled;
its lower end is sunk in murky slime.
She sets her smartphone up – to show the world –
and then, with nonchalance, begins her climb.

A stripling lass, who's armed with two bare hands,
she urges me to prod so he swims close
for her to grab. Although she understands
his venom sac contains a lethal dose,

she seems to be completely unconcerned.
As he swims past, she catches at his tail.
Her expertise is clear, her craft well learned,
but still I give a shudder, lest she fail.

The bane of age is caution; there's the truth.
It is the gulf dividing age from youth.

7

It is the gulf dividing age from youth.
Our fears intensify with passing time.
Though we may think our juniors are uncouth,
they sometimes show that we are past our prime.

I capped the price of freedom. Was that right?
I let my fear dictate a course to take
and nearly stooped to murder out of fright.
A younger heart shone light on my mistake,

and gave me cause to think, to ruminate
on why we're here. Compassion came to mind;
a virtue that I've sometimes lost of late.
The world's a better place when we are kind.

I asked her what the snake now had in store.
'Release,' she said, 'into a habitat
away from human dwellings, to explore
its native bushland, growing old and fat,

away from foolish humans who cause strife.
This snake that came was only seeking life.'

A Double Rainbow in New York

The brownstone buildings, tall, austere,
match morbid skies that scowl and lour.
Such days as this are drab and drear,
for this is not a passing shower.

When maudlin thoughts I cannot quell,
a double rainbow can inspire
such joy and hope that will dispel
all gloom, and set my heart on fire.

While nature's second bow is pale,
like words within a palimpsest,
a human child can blaze a trail,
when of maternal love possessed.

Her footsteps are the pot of gold
on which her mother's love is sold.

The Bee

A swirl of half-chewed hay, and on it clings
one drowning bee, whose struggle seems in vain;
a poor bedraggled thing with sodden wings,
but how she fights for life as her strength wanes.

For pity's sake, I take a length of wood
and lift her from the trough, onto the side,
where, in the sun, it seems perhaps she could
revive. She washes while her wings are dried.

Her jointed legs brush moisture from her head,
meticulous, and with exacting care.
She tries her wings; a sudden vibrant spread
of gossamer beats hard upon the air,

in drunken flight, as is my heart, set free
as home I trudge – to honey for my tea.

Dawn at Guichen Bay

Before the dawn, when all is dark and still,
magenta tints are spread across the arc
of this fair bay. They slowly turn to gold.
A breeze springs up to lift the veil away,
with sudden freshness that assaults the nose.

Grey seagulls, mirrored in the sea-glazed sand,
strut up and down the beach on sticks for legs.
They peck round turban shells of mottled green,
for doors not closed to save the snails within,
then arch their necks, and lunge at morsels cast
ashore upon the gentle to and fro.

Small scallop shells are lifted by the tide
and soft, insistent nudge of swirling surf,
where carmine strands of weed drift listlessly,
erasing three-pronged tracks of dainty birds.

I clamber over limestone rocks, to watch
clouds tinged with pink against a duck egg sky.
A sudden wave throws up a diamond spray,
just as the rising sun begins to spill
a blazing shimmer path across the waves;

a tempting path to take when my time comes,
but while the clock still ticks, I am enthralled.

Sulphur-crested Cockatoos

The screeching cockatoos in hundreds swoop,
avenging angels at the trump of doom,
with fanned white wings, backlit like skeins of lace;
a wheeling flock above the river's course.

Their sulphur crests on fire against the sun;
unsettled, as they throng round undrowned trees,
on whose gaunt limbs they shift, like candle flames
at mumbled evensong, in muted tones.

Dusk softly fades in blushes, rose and pink,
and squabbles soon subside to peacefulness.
All now is silent on the billabong,
but tiny splashes heard as bell frogs leap.

Small sparkling gems adorn the velvet dome,
attendant on the silent, rising moon.

The Weavers

Those who knew the ancient lore
of lake and shore,
wove their rushes long before
the white man came.

Shallow baskets scooped up fish,
their staple dish;
winnowed grain with rhythmic swish,
till white man came.

With artistry, they wove mats
where elders sat
in woven cloaks, shielding backs
from white man's claim.

In their weaving, each stitch told,
in every fold,
Dreamtime tales that earned the cold
white man's disdain.

With the coming of the cloud,
their wisdom cowed,
folded in each woven shroud,
to white man's shame.

Remaining reeds whisper soft
the grievous cost
of the weavers' wisdom lost
when white man came.

The Secret of the Rose

In summer sun the buds unfurl.
As her pubescent beauty grows,
I pluck such buds to tempt my girl;
I know the secret of the rose.

I woo her with its heady scent;
it brings more joy than you'd suppose.
This pheromone's on pleasure bent;
I know the secret of the rose.

As lips unite, our love to seal,
her petals fall, her heart's exposed,
and, as her swelling hips reveal,
I know the secret of the rose.

Our passion's child will soon be born,
and with kid gloves, I will enclose
the hidden dangers of the thorn;
I know the secret of the rose.

The Seven-tined Stag

The forest's filled with magic on this night.
Huntsman, take care! Beware of giving chase,
else you may find yourself the helpless prey.

Shadows confuse the margins of this place,
enticing those whose will is weak, to stray,
violating realms where laws of time and space
extend and then implode like dying stars.
No man returns who heeds the call of fate.

There, in the twilight, stands the seven-tined stag,
its outline sharp against the close of day,
noble in its form, its nostrils flared.
Erin's legends warn that its changeling shape,
deludes, seducing humanfolk away.

Stand firm in faith, lest fooled by artifice
that's filled with empty promise of delight.
Avoid this apparition, for it's fey!
Good huntsman, seal your eyes and ears tonight.

Consider the Oyster

Consider the oyster,
by fate inflamed,
who, reaching within,
wraps pearl around pain.

Tilting at Windmills

How wildly wind-shanked windows rattle,
the terror of the banshee battle,
the storm surge seeps through weeping cracks,
to tear apart established facts.

But encased in faith's dull armour,
blood-crusted in pursuit of right,
this old crusader, resurrected,
stands ready, resolute to fight.

Once more unto the battledore,
to loft his shuttlecock of shame,
but how the howling gale is blowing
through his wormwood weakened frame.

Since his armour's rather rusted,
ancient rites no longer trusted,
he is tempted by the devil
to genuflect, and then skedaddle.

When Inspiration Strikes

When inspiration strikes, full steam ahead!
Seize brushes with both hands, before it's fled.
Spread out the paper's blank – no time to lose –
and plunge into the yellows, reds and blues.
Speed's of the essence, lest you lose the thread.

Unleash your latent mind, from A to Zed,
ignite the inner spark before it's dead,
it's only fools who stop to take a snooze
                when inspiration strikes!

It pays you to be quick, not filled with dread.
Embrace your muse with love if you'd be wed;
make her an offering she can't refuse.
The moment's now, and only you can choose
how you go down the path on which you're led
                when inspiration strikes!

The Harp

Awake the seven sleeping strings
to plink soft rills of sound,
a fluttering like butterflies,
above the elven mound.

A faerie spirit born of breath,
trapped in a netted tree,
beats fragile wings of gossamer,
frantic to be free.

Now comes a vibrant rush of wind,
Aeolus' bag unleashed,
scattering the tattered mesh,
and thus is Sith released.

Awake the breaking roll of waves,
let fingers writhe and stall,
resolving mounting dissonance
as notes dissolve and fall.

The sky is filled with restless dead
escaped from mortal form,
to search the shores of otherworld
in music's pulse, forlorn.

Yet let us weave arpeggios
that splash like sunlit spume,
as selkies sport in sandy coves
to tease away the gloom;

and they shall sing till day goes down
on water's mystic sway,
so put aside your minstrelsy,
and dance with them, away.

Amongst the Stars

Set amongst the stars,
tinged with immortality,
this great love of ours,
breaches death's infinity,
urgently impelling birth.

Stars descend to earth,
silver shards that quell the night,
measureless in worth,
ecstasy and pure delight,
tempting hearts to join in bliss.

Though heaven's abyss
stretches out beyond the main,
wavering's amiss!
Let us flee your father's men,
and strive boldly to retain

this great love of ours,
set amongst the stars.

The Pool

I hear the silent pool; its rippled sigh
stirs up the muddied depths of memory.
The slender reeds vibrate with whispered songs
of you and mayfly moments, long since gone.
A swish of fins, a sudden swirl, and splash!
The fragile damsel's lost – a rainbow flash.
Concentric circles spread to lap the shore
before the troubled pond is still once more.

The heron's slender figure etched in greys,
blinks at the ballet legs that hold my gaze,
and then, with lunging speed, he thrusts his lance
to pin the skimming dancer in mid-dance,
just as the fateful sword took you that day,
and casual, lazy wings bore life away.

Ruminations

Her liquid eye holds dreams
of chaff twice chewed
and that's enough
to fill the stomach of her mind.
How deep need ruminations be?

Between those horns there lies
the bovine essence of eternity;
contentment, chewing cud,
like you or me.

Yet we who fence her field
of winter hay,
will send her, in due course,
to the slaughterhouse.

Will deeper thinking make her more secure
or happier?

Annealed by Fire

Her life in tatters,
lost, and ash
concealing just the twisted knife,
a melted pot,
and bones;
calcified remains on which to build
the framework of a life again.

I saw her face, annealed by fire,
grey-haired and gaunt, with lilac eye.
She gripped her spade,
and then began to dig;
such strength as this our women have.

The Bells

Sound words like bells
in blacksmith's forge,
each chime a shuddering hour
that fades;
hours of iron,
once strong and brave,
on warhorse hooves;

their muffled thud through damp, loam woods –
a sound that's lost in russet ooze
as soldiers seek oblivion.

At length, a few return
on metalled roads;
their ears still ring
with words and deeds
that will be told, and tolled
in mournful carillon,

each widowed word wrung out in grief,
then spread across the world.

The Sleeping Music

The sleeping music lies
in harmonies of stream
and spring and waterfall;
glissandos into pools
where quiet waters swirl,
and leaves stirred by the evening breeze
perform a *pas de deux*.

When silken skies subside,
enchanted,
gold and rose,
their glow embalms
the sallow flesh of day
and calms each bruise,

till in sleep I'm drowned
with echoes of those
whose shadows form,
like flotsam
on the dead sea swell;
fragmented figures from the past,
now bereft of sound.

Night Ode

The light is drowned tonight
beneath a turquoise sea.

All colour fades to black,
the world lies still,
falls cold,
and calls the darkness
out of me.

What slight shadows
cloud my mind,
when set against
the vastness of the void
beyond the shapes we see.

Yet, with their darkness gone,
I've space
and time to think
without the thrall of day,
discerning now the part,
though it be small,
that I shall choose to play.

Beyond the Wit of Daylight Hours

I have wandered in dark places,
and sought reflection in silent pools
bathed in moonlight,

on paths beyond the wit
of daylight hours,

and there have found
in solitude
the truth in dreams,
the music of deeper worlds than ours,
a confluence with faerie land

that, in kindness,
binds us to ourselves
and to our clay,
when comes the newborn day
and leaves such echoes
as do haunt the song of birds
and mists that rise from dew;

a bidding to fare well,
as blow the winds into
the fleeting sails
of friendship
found each day anew
in ancient grains of sand
and pulsing veins.

Going Home

The coo of pigeons calls me back
to leaf mould damp
and watered sun
that glistens on the turning leaves
of childhood memory
where lone I walk through time.

I see the lithesome hips of rose;
a blackbird poised
on rusted rail of iron
entwined with old man's beard;
and bones long gone.
The church bell chimes.

The hour of evensong has come.
I kneel
and peep between the steeple of my hands
at sandstone arches stained
by saints in glowing robes
whose scarlet hues and sad eyes fall
on chiselled names of those
who passed this way before.

The Advent candle flickers
in the fading light of day,
a rose-rimmed eye that blinks
and forces out a waxen tear
for those, my kin, who died.

In His Own Image

Beware the gods that man himself has made,
his idle speculations carved in stone,
erecting prohibitions that proscribe
free minds and thought, with reasoning that's just

designed from faith, blind faith adorned with pomp,
and filigreed in guilt, a tracery
etched deep with shibboleths and sacrifice,
inquisitive for tortured lies and fear.

Where is the love in this that good men sought;
that gift, imagined in creation's flame?

Through Gritted Teeth

Forgive me if my love is not complete
for there are those I simply cannot stand.
Is it enough I do not wish them harm
and when I meet them treat them with respect?
Is it enough that I am not unkind,
and in my dealings, I remain humane?
Though courtesy comes cheap, it can mean much,
I therefore try to keep aversions hid
and subjugate the words I have in mind,
but when I say fare well, I really mean farewell!

Sirocco

Three clouds disturb a pale blue sky;
a beard, a bird, an angel's eye,
prepare to flee the sandstorm wind,
that whips against the tamarind,

abraded beard consumes the bird,
the angel blinks a tumbled word,
loose shutters slam against the fear
while wolf cubs cower in their lair

and whimper as their mothers howl.
A gust picks up a Leghorn fowl;
white feathers fly against the wind
like prayers for mercy when we've sinned.

Too late, too late, the mountains moan,
the aspens bend, their branches groan,
Sirocco sweeps our lies away,
dissembled clouds, in disarray.

The Old Violin

What fine tunes can be played on an old violin
when her strings are deranged by a strong slender bow
that can draw from her heart the original sin
of a swift gypsy dance, as she sways to and fro,

and the chattering shake of the shrill tambourine
underlines with its thrill the wild notes of desire
that are drawn from her depths, as we hear her songs keen
to the castanets' clicking that sets men on fire.

Oh, the chords she lets fall in her fervid disgrace
may awaken faint echoes in ancients who sin –
in their dreams – whilst in turn, younger *beaux* take their place
to derange the wild strings of an old violin.

When Leaves are Fish

It's poetry that feeds the soul.
A poet fishes in the trees,
though other fish may fill our bowl,
his silver minnows catch the breeze.

A poet fishes in the trees,
the words he uses take us where
his silver minnows catch the breeze
to banish all our thoughts of care.

The words he uses take us where
the phosphorescent sea sprites dance
to banish all our thoughts of care
on moonlit nights where lovers chance

the phosphorescent sea sprites' dance,
and we may feast on honeyed words
on moonlit nights where lovers chance
to sing their poems wild as birds.

And we may feast on honeyed words
that lift our hearts and make us wish
to sing their poems wild as birds.
Our fancy flies when leaves are fish

that lift our hearts and make us wish.
Though other fish may fill our bowl,
our fancy flies when leaves are fish.
It's poetry that feeds the soul.

Our Late Milkman

Today the milkman's running late
I wonder why?
If he turned up, it would be great.
Have cows run dry?
My irritation turns to guilt.
I rarely grieve when milk is spilt
But this occasion made me cry.
You wonder why?

It was a tragic twist of fate
that cast the die.
He swerved. The 'roo made its escape.
A truck came by
around a corner that was blind.
A wife, two children, left behind.
The fates have crushed one lovely guy.
I wonder why?

Those Who Watch and Wait

Such storms have scarred this ancient coast on many nights before
and lashed the jagged moonlit rocks with shattered pearls of spray.
Dark monsters of the deep now hurl their shards of spite ashore,
while chill winds whip the harbour wall that holds the waves at bay

and, bearing up against this roar of elemental rage
two sentinels of timeless stone, beyond all bounds of fear,
defy the salted wounds of seas that are their daily wage.
They watch in hope, and in that hope, hold back a silent tear.

A mother and her child stand there, eroded by their grief,
like other wives who through the years have waited thus in vain
sustained in life alone on shore by virtue of belief
that they one day with joy will see their loved ones home again.

For it is hope that carries us, when faced with storms each day,
and helps us gather shattered pearls to build our dreams once more.
If we keep faith with those we love, though they be far away,
we have the power, when tempests rage, to dream them safe to shore.

The Superb Fairy Wren

It's time to shed my drab brown coat!
To win a mate, I need some flair!
I'll don a cap of brilliant blue,
a mantle made to match, and wear
a mask of black to patch the eye
of Scaramouche, the debonair!

My pencil tail erectly stands;
I strut to show I have no fear;
to add panache, I call Prrp! Prrp!
to challenge rival males who dare.
They call me Fairy Wren in jest,
but there was never wren more fair!

Good God! What upstart wretch is this
who ponces in the looking glass?
I'll have at him and drive him off
and send him packing. Silly arse!
The bounder apes my every move!
What cheek! Tsee! No more this farce!

He flapped his wings and launched attack
in reckless flight, ferociously.
He threw himself against the glass
with battle cry: Tsee! Tsee!
His mimic flew with equal force,
and hit as hard, but silently.

The battle raged for half an hour;
our six-inch hero showed no fear.
A mate looked on and fancied him;
aroused, she fluttered round to share
our hero's nest. 'Not now,' he peeped,
'I have an aching head, my dear!'

Brave Robert

Such tears of laughter, tears of joy
were wept upon this lovely boy.
He was a cheerful little chap,
which sometimes saved him from the strap.

Tears often flowed, it's sad to say,
when Robert did not get his way,
and at those times his father said,
'Now dry those eyes and off to bed!'

When nightmares breeched his inner fears,
his parents wiped away his tears;
they saved him from emotion's wave;
they soothed and hushed him: 'Son, be brave!'

They gave him Christmas games of war,
bright leaden soldiers on the floor.
He came of age and joined the ranks
to play with somewhat larger tanks.

The banter in the barrack room
brought tears of laughter, not of doom,
but even so he dried his eye;
it was ingrained; real men don't cry.

In coming days, his best mates died.
He kept his tears locked up inside.
They swamped his heart without a sound.
His eye stayed dry, but he was drowned.

The Eagle

I watched an eagle hover, spill the air
from wings outstretched and pause from languid flight.
Such fine control and majesty were there
as made my spirit soar, and gaining height,

it sought to capture him upon a page
and pinion him in measured words of ink
that poets use to form a gilded cage
when beauty makes them pause awhile to think.

But caged, their thoughts sublime no longer fly
like eagles high above the world of men.
Such spirits chained no longer soar. They die
unless a reader gives them flight again.

Imagination can unchain the words
and turn them once again to soaring birds.

Self-sufficiency

You ask of me a thing I baulk to give;
confessionals of love are private land,
and yet you ask that I should publicise
In verse my weaknesses for all the world.
Does not the player have a right to wear
a mask to hide the man behind the part?
So much of what I am is deep submerged
behind a mask I grew at boarding school
to hide the way I felt and to conform
to norms that lay within unwritten lore.

A dozen years of this from age of six
was time enough to print a mould on me
of self-sufficiency that stood me well
for years in squadron service for the Queen,
until I reached the age of thirty-eight
and left my native land and safety net;
a happy choice that put me in free fall;

a new Australian land, new family
and back to school to gain a new degree;
four years to learn to teach, to teach to learn,
the only job three hundred miles away.
So, three more years, by road four hours apart,
your mother left to hold the fort alone
with little help from me. I was not there
except most fleetingly, and once again
I wore a mask of self-sufficiency,
a mask that hid deep sadness as I saw
your days of early childhood slip away.
It was a Janus mask; one face looked back
at family, the other one ahead,
to carve a niche within a new career.

A Winter Gale

Dark trees that danced macabre through the night
still shake in frantic palsy at first light;
the huff and buffet on the windowpane
impels in gusts the sudden stinging rain.
There are no colours in the dawn today;
the world is cast in dismal shades of grey,

So, too, my mood when winter shows its fist.
I far prefer the stealth of morning mist
with pallid sunlight seeping gently through,
intent on drying elfin tears of dew
and warming dormant bulbs that lie abed
like me, enjoying dreams of spring ahead.

The Mermaid

Now storms have ceased and sailing days are done
and gentle ripples lap the coral shore.
His mermaid's just a shadow in the sun
but still as tempting as she was before.

Yes, still he dreams of flying on the breeze
along the molten path the sun gods spread
to light her female form, that it might tease
with limbs of gold and turn a sailor's head.

He hauled on sheets in hope, with lovelorn sighs,
and set the sails that drove him to despair
on granite rocks, instead of yielding thighs.
Thus mermaids treat the man who comes in fear,

but when we scale the rocks we do not fail.
It's when we lose our heads, we win the grail.

Rainbow Lorikeets

The sun-flecked sea dissembles harmony
until a shot rings out across the sand
disturbing raucous rainbows from a tree

and as they rise, with ruffled feathers fanned,
a sudden cloud of chatter fills the air.
They circle, glide in slowly, then they land.

When satisfied that danger is not near,
these lorikeets resume their search for food
and squawk their petty squabbles, free from fear.

Bedecked in gaudy colours, many-hued,
they preen and promenade, now safe once more
and pecking order postures cause a feud.

We too will flock and fluster when guns roar;
safe, we settle back, pecking as before.

Teenage Angst

We had fifteen years of joy and some tears.
Your journey printed, etched upon the heart,
sharing your hopes, allaying all your fears,
begrudging each minute we were apart –
we did our best to give you a good start.

How did we feel when you went your own way
on paths that would break you if they held sway?
Helpless in all but the strength of our love,
but that you foreswore and held us at bay
with Damocles' sword unsteady above,

held over our heads and ready to fall.
In your rush for freedom at any price,
you ignored the risk of destroying all
as you wavered beneath the gnawing mice
that weakened the thread. Life ends in a trice.

If you have children, you'll know how it feels;
how, when they are threatened, the blood congeals;
to what lengths you'd go to protect your child;
what joy it is when the strength of love heals
tears in the fabric – and you're reconciled.

Gungalo

The stillness of a sheoak grove at night
is woken by a whispered tropic breeze
and shivers with a sigh in soft moonlight
as zephyrs stroke the heartstrings of the trees,

and scriven songs of love upon the bark.
Within this sound I hear her voice again;
it sings her songs of love despite the dark
that stole the kiss of this, her last refrain.

Her heart held still such store of songs to sing
before her gentle breath expired in sighs,
and she was lifted on an angel's wing
to carry on her work in Paradise.

The songs she left step softly through my mind;
her words impressed like footprints left behind.

The Duet

Play me a tune, string me along,
I am entranced by every trill.
This is my heart, swathe it in song,
pluck at the strings, give me a thrill.
If truly you love me, you will.

My tune, my love, is a duet,
your voice also needed, my pet,
the chords of our hearts are as one.
I'll sing our song without regret
if you will sing too till we're done.

Family

Family is an accretion of small memories
to build a coral reef of love
if we are patient,

or a wall of misunderstanding
with hearts beating on either side
if we are not.

The Blue Period

Picasso had a Blue Period
when he painted prostitutes, beggars and drunks
in various shades of blue
and became quite unpopular
because of it.
My daughter and I had a Blue Period
when we painted a bedroom with towels
soaked in blue paint,
which we threw at the walls
and at each other.
The results were quite amazing.
We, too, were unpopular.

Paper Tigers

We exchanged paper tigers
in the dark days
Of the Kurt Cobain addiction,
neither understanding the other;
I, still enmeshed in the cocoon of her childhood,
she, struggling to emerge
and test her newfound wings.
Never mind that
exotic night flowers are poisoned
and enticing flames burn,
For we must all learn to fly.
It took time for me to learn
that she must write her own life
in free, unrhymed verse,
not the straitjacket of the formal sonnet
so much preferred by her parent.

The Old Quarry

Up on the hill there is a house of stone
whose heart is carved from rocks wrenched from the ground.
It stands foursquare, aloof and all alone,
arising from the land to which it's bound.
Its craftsmen, though long dead and now unknown,
still dwell within its walls, and still the sound
of hammers haunts the reaches of the night;
each stone hand-picked to lock the others tight.

The quarry lies a short stroll up the dene.
Its guts, torn from the belly of the hill,
left jagged scars, a miniature ravine,
but Nature now conceals the violent spill
with brambles, boxthorn and a salve of green,
a haven for small birds that flit, then still
their wing, alert for feral cat and fox,
and hawks that hover, high above the rocks.

Its stone-girt pool holds deep and ancient thoughts
concealed beneath the virid algal bloom,
secreted through the jagged lines of quartz
to cool this place and soothe away that gloom
that grips at times. Its silence soon transports
the mind from worldly troubles and small fears,
displacing them with solitude and calm;
a secret healing place on Brooklands farm.

www.ingramcontent.com/pod-product-compliance
Lightning Source LLC
Chambersburg PA
CBHW070919080526
44589CB00013B/1359